Donated by
Ryan Parsons

D1561195

*Presented to*

_____

*from*

_____

_____  *19*___

# The King's Animals

## A Bible Book about God's Creatures

*Other Books in the*
*Children of the King Series:*

*The King's Alphabet*
A Bible Book About Letters

*The King's Numbers*
A Bible Book About Counting

*The King's Manners*
A Bible Book About Courtesy

*The King's Workers*
A Bible Book About Serving

*The King's Children*
A Bible Book About God's People

Managing Editor: Laura Minchew
Project Editor: Brenda Ward

**The King's Animals**
Copyright © 1991 by WORD Publishing

**Library of Congress Cataloging-in-Publication Data**

Hollingsworth, Mary, 1947-
The King's animals : a Bible book about God's creatures / illustrated
by Mary Grace Eubank : text by Mary Hollingsworth.
p. cm. — (The Children of the King series)
"Word kids!"
Summary: Whimsical rhymes introduce many of the animals
of the world and the God who created them all.
ISBN 0-8499-0907-4
[1. Animals–Fiction. 2. Christian life–Fiction. 3. Stories in rhyme.]
I. Eubank, Mary Grace, ill. II. Title. III. Series: Hollingsworth,
Mary, 1947-
Children of the King series.
PZ8.3.H7196Kig 1991
[E] — dc20                                          91-19093
                                                        CIP
                                                        AC
Printed in the United States of America
12349LB987654321

# The King's Animals

## A Bible Book about God's Creatures

Illustrated by: Mary Grace Eubank
Text by: Mary Hollingsworth

WORD PUBLISHING
Dallas · London · Vancouver · Melbourne

'Twas in the spring
The kindly king
Set up the royal circus ring.
"Let trapeze swing!
Let's laugh and sing
And watch the fun my critters bring."

A rabbit from Kent
Walked into the tent
As Ring Master for the event.
To the center he went,
"Now, ladies and gents,
The King's Circus we proudly present!"

A whistle's tweet
Began the beat
Of music grand and sweet,
Then happy feet
(Oh, what a treat!)
Marched past the kingly seat.

A dancing bear
(I do declare!)
Balanced a ball in the air.
But you beware —
God made the bear
To "Growl!" and give a scare.

Giraffe came by
With head so high
It almost touched God's sky.
Though quiet and shy,
She'd always try
To wink at Butterfly.

Two very nice
Small German mice
Sold lemonade with ice,
And twice as nice,
At half the price,
Were a Coke and pizza slice.

A poodle troop
Was led by Roop
And ran around a loop.
Their ears might droop,
But what a group —
They jump from hoop to hoop!

On God's elegant
Lady elephant
Rode glorious Lola Van Zandt.
Her charming chant
Was grand, I grant
But her size made the elephant pant.

Then fancy and big,
Sweet Prissy Pig
Came wearing a thingumajig,
She held her wig
And danced a jig
Like a spinning whirligig.

Then Minnie Lou,
God's Kangaroo,
In a purple tennis shoe,
Played peekaboo
With the king: "Yoohoo!"
I'd do it too; would you?

Now, look at this,
And don't you miss
God's snake called Mister Swiss.
Enjoy his "hiss,"
But listen, Sis,
Avoid his snaky kiss.

Then with a "quack"
Came Good News Jack,
A duck from Hackensack.
He rode piggyback
On the back of Yak
Whose hooves went clackety-clack.

A monkey named Flyer
Climbed higher and higher
To ride on a swaying high wire.
An act to admire,
He rode through a fire
On his unicycle with a flat tire!

A tiger named Jink
And his pal, Humperdinck,
Growled a trio with Martin the Mink.
Then the king gave a wink
For he liked it, I think,
And the tigers both blushed pretty pink.

God's owl, Cahoot,
In a pink-sequinned suit,
Played a tune on his flute.
In top hat and boot,
He was really quite cute
Snapping the king a salute.

A flock of geese
That came from Greece,
Led by a goose named Bernice,
"Honked" a loud piece
Titled "God's Perfect Peace,"
'Til the king shouted out, "Please cease!"

Then out of the blue
Came a marvelous "Moo!"
And Gertrude the cow came in view.
With a "How do you do!"
And a sweet "Toodle-oo,"
She marched in the tent and on through.

Ginger the cat
In her bright yellow hat
Came marching right next to Sir Rat.
Now, a cat and a rat
Quite naturally spat,
But not in this show — how 'bout that?

Flapper Seal
Had great appeal
Diving with Ollie the eel.
His fishy meal
Made Flapper feel
Like clapping his fins with zeal!

Behind them came Flora
In red-plumed fedora
Beside her twin sister, Lenora.
Lenora and Flora,
From south Bora Bora,
"Brayed" and "hee hawed" out the door-a.

A giant "Roar"!
Announced Old Thor —
God's lion ambassador.
He's brave, and what's more,
He can even outroar
Bohanan, the great dinosaur.

God's rooster named Jot
From Old Hottentot,
"Ca-ca-doodle-dood" quite a lot,
But he forgot
To crow or not
When out of a cannon he shot!

Next was seen Evangelene,
God's sheep and
meadow queen.
Her cape was green —
Silk gabardine! —
And she played
a mean tambourine.

With a noisy "neigh"
Came dancing Ray —
A horse from west L.A.
The tent would sway
As he tapped away,
And folks shouted, "Hip hooray!"

Rusty the hound,
Dressed up as a clown,
Rode his red bike 'round and 'round.
The king lost his frown
When the dog tumbled down,
Turning flip-flops on the ground.

At last, Madam Tess,
A hippo from Kress,
Dropped down in a blue satin dress.
She was happy, oh yes,
To hear the king bless
The animals' circus success.

Then the king's cheer
Was easy to hear —
He clapped, and he grinned ear to ear.
And he was sincere
When he said soft but clear,
"Bless every animal here."